C0-BIG-972

The Vacation

by Michèle Dufresne

Pioneer Valley Educational Press, Inc.

Dad, Mom, Nick, and Matt are going on a vacation.

"Look, here is a plane," said Nick.

"Oh, no!" said Dad.
"Oh, no!"

"Come on," said Mom.

"Come on, Dad," said Matt.

"Look, Dad! Come up here,"
said Nick and Matt.

"Oh, no!" said Dad.
"Oh, no!"

"Look, Dad!" said Nick.
"Here is a cave."

"Oh, no!" said Dad.
"Oh, no!"

"Look! A boat," said Matt.
"Here is a boat!"

"Oh, no!" said Dad.
"No, no, no."

"Oh, look," said Dad. "Here is a beach."

"Oh, yes, yes, yes," said Dad.
"I like the beach."